One Rehearsal WONDERS

ALMOST INSTANT ANTHEMS FOR ANY OCCASION

CONTENTS:

GlorySound

EXCLUSIVELY DISTRIBUTED BY

HAL•LEONARD®
CORPORATION
7777 W. BLUEMOUND RD. P.O. BOX 13819 MILWAUKEE, WI 53213

Visit Shawnee Press Online at **www.shawneepress.com**

From the Publisher...

This exciting potpourri of praise is a collection of excellent anthems especially chosen for their ability to be easily and quickly learned. Special care was taken to include worship resources that sound rich and full, even in SAB and two-part formats.

In this compilation of best-sellers, you will find festive calls to purpose and songs of grace and comfort. There are gospel and contemporary pieces along with more traditional musical styles. There are tender songs of thanksgiving and inspiring sounds of encouragement and hope. These anthems contain messages that challenge the heart spiritually, but are musically accessible to choirs of every size and level of ability.

In conjunction with this collection, we are pleased to introduce a new product we call iPrint. Contained on this special CD-ROM are reproducible instrumental scores for almost all of the anthems in the book. These will often include guitar and bass guitar charts, as well as obligato parts when appropriate. As you listen to the demo recording of these anthems, you may be inspired to have your own musicians provide backup for your choir. In each case, the parts are written with sensitivity to churches with limited resources and are arranged to insure successful performances by your developing instrumentalists. Whether you use piano, the accompaniment CD, or make use of our iPrint instrumental parts, we hope that having these options will enable you to meet the needs of your community of faith.

I WILL REJOICE

for S.A.B. voices, accompanied

Based on
Habakkuk 3:18

Words and Music by
JOSEPH M. MARTIN
(BMI)

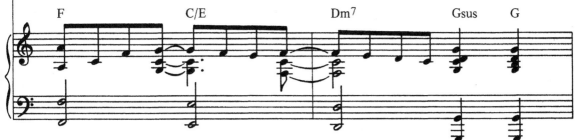

6

I will fol - low where you lead. ____

I will fol - low where you lead, where you lead. ____

Ab/Eb   Eb   Bb/Eb   Eb

43 *mf cresc. poco a poco*   *with increasing excitement*

Set me, Lord, to high - er plac - es;

mf cresc. poco a poco

To high - er plac - es;

43 E/B   A/B   E/B

mf cresc. poco a poco   *with increasing excitement*

lift me high so I can see

lift me high so I can see, I can see ____

A/B   B   E/B

10

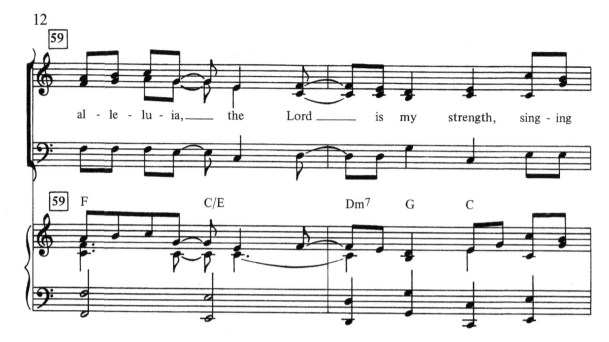

al - le - lu - ia,___ the Lord ___ is my strength, sing - ing

al - le - lu - ia,___ the Lord is my strength.

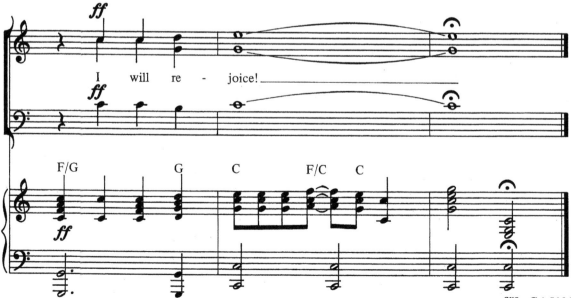

I will re - joice!___

8va GA5101

HE WILL CARRY YOU THROUGH

for 2-part mixed voices, accompanied*

Words by
JENNIFER DOWELL (ASCAP)

Music by
MICHAEL BARRETT (BMI)

Gently rhythmic (♩ = ca. 108-112)

but my friend, there's hope in Jesus' precious name.

When you are re-ject-ed,

look to the One who died

when you turn a-way,

*Quoting text from "Yield Not to Temptation"; Text: H.R. Palmer (1834-1907)

He is will - ing to aid ___ you. ___

2nd time to Coda ✦, p. 8

He will car - ry you through. ___

2nd time to Coda ✦, p. 8

He will car - ry you through. _

Those who are search - ing, _ those who've gone a-stray, _

seek His king - dom _ first, _ and you will

ONE STEP HE LEADS

for S.A.T.B. voices, accompanied*

Words and Music by
PEPPER CHOPLIN (ASCAP)

In a triplet feel (♩ = ca. 92)

ACCOMP.

SOPRANO & ALTO UNISON

Some-times I wor-ry and wish I could see what lies a - head, what the fu-ture will be. But

GA5101

13 God calls me on to fol-low in faith, and

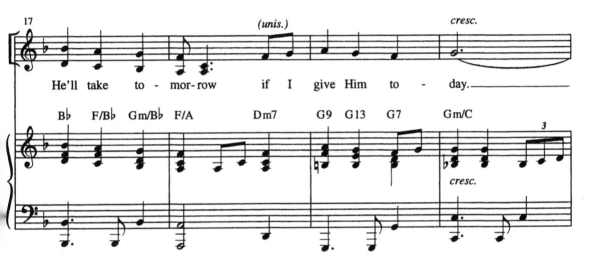

He'll take to-mor-row if I give Him to - day.

(unis.) *cresc.*

One step He leads and one step I'll

TENOR

BASS

mf

fol - low, God knows my needs and He will sup - ply. I don't know the fu - ture and all that's in store, so I'll take one step, one step to fol - low my

Lord.

Je - sus said,

"Leave all your wor-ries,— for-get all your cares,"

What you will— eat and what you will wear. But

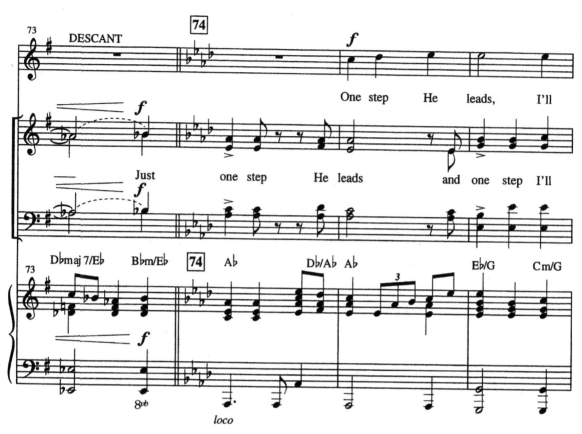

to the Chancel Choir of
Peninsula-McCabe United Methodist Church, Wilmington, Delaware

PRAISE GOD!

for S.A.B.* voices, accompanied**

Arranged by
DON BESIG (ASCAP)

Words and Music by
ROBERT T. McALPINE

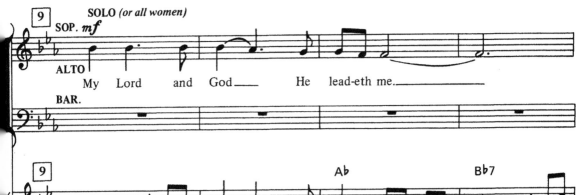

A5101

He is my strength ev - 'ry day, _____

SOLO *(or all men)* **mf**

ev - 'ry day. _____

Eb/G   Ab   Fm7/Bb   Bb

When I am filled _____ with hope-less-ness, _____

Eb   Eb/G Ab

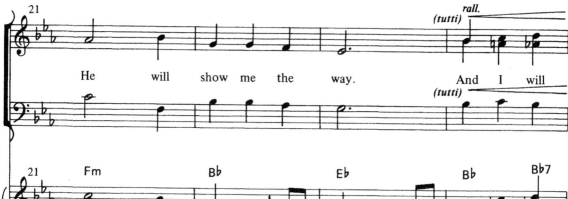

rall.
(tutti)

He will show me the way.   And I will

(tutti)

Fm   Bb   Eb   Bb   Bb7

rall.

praise the Lord my God by the morn-ing light._____ And I will

praise God, praise God,

praise the Lord my God ___ ev-'ry night. ___

I know that my God is filled with love. ___

praise God, praise God,

praise the Lord my God by the morn-ing light. _____ And I will

praise God, praise God,

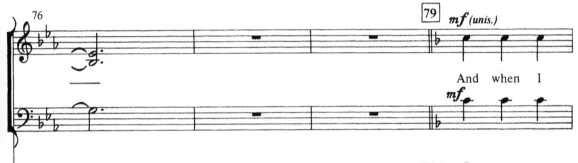

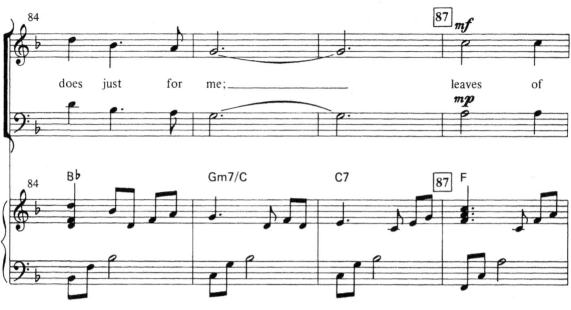

praise God, praise God,

praise the Lord my God by the morn-ing light.____

And I will praise God, praise

38

* one voice on top note

Delight Yourself in the Lord

for S.A.B. voices, accompanied*

Words by
J. PAUL WILLIAMS (ASCAP)

Music by
MICHAEL BARRETT (BMI)

Joyfully (♩ = ca. 138)

Accomp.

mf

SOPRANO (unis.) *mf*

ALTO

BARITONE *mf*

De - light your-self __ in the Lord. Com -

mit your way __ un - to Him. The Lord will sus-tain __ and al -

40

GA510

light your-self __ in the Lord.

Re - fresh your - self in streams of right - eous - ness. _____

De - pend on His un - chang - ing Word.

_____ your-self _ in the Lord. De - light in the Lord. _

Lord. Let hearts be filled _ with His praise. Step

re - joice in the Light. _ De - light your-self _ in the

out of your night, _

Lord. De - light your- self _ in the Lord!

(div.)

Awaken Me To Pray

for S.A.B. voices, accompanied*

Words by
JOHN PARKER (ASCAP)

Music by
DAVID LANTZ III (ASCAP)

Lyrics: A- wak-en me to pray, O my Fa - ther, when the night is long, O my Lord.

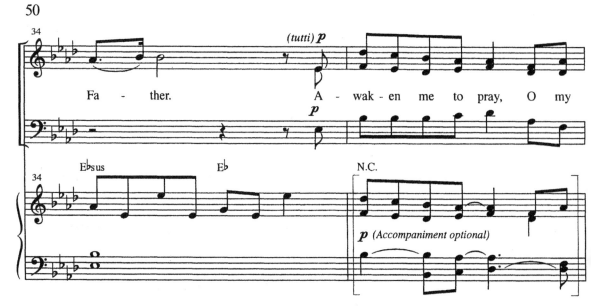

Fa - ther. A - wak - en me to pray, O my Lord.

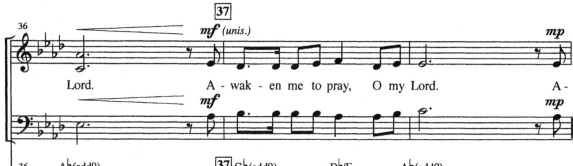

Lord. A - wak - en me to pray, O my Lord. A -

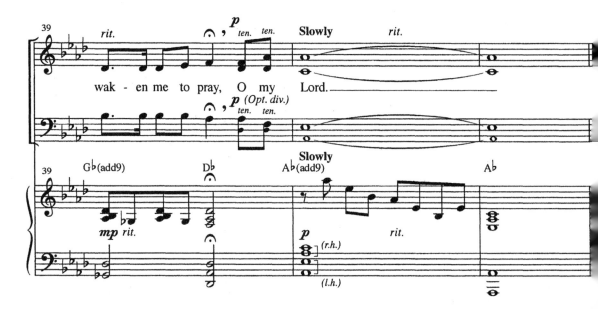

wak - en me to pray, O my Lord.

O GIVE THANKS

S.A.B. voices, accompanied

Based on
PSALM 105:1-5

Words and Music by
JOSEPH M. MARTIN
(BMI)

A5101

things that He has done. Come and call up-on His Name,—

Ebm   Ebm/Ab   Db   Ab/C

—— ev-'ry na-tion now pro-claim,—— O give thanks,— give your

Bbm   Db/Ab   Gb   Db/F

hon-or to the Lord, O give thanks.

Ebm7   Ab   Db   Ab/Db   Gb   Ebm/Ab

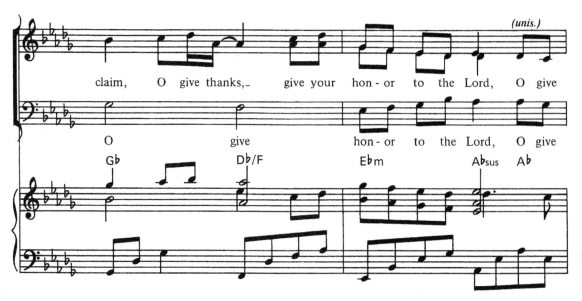

(unis.)

claim, O give thanks,_ give your hon - or to the Lord, O give

O give hon - or to the Lord, O give

Gb   Db/F   Ebm   Absus Ab

thanks.

thanks._

Dbsus   Db   Dbsus   Db

25

mf

O give thanks to Him,

mf

O give thanks to Him who rides up - on the wind._

25

Bbm   Fm7   Gb   Db/F

mf

cresc.

peo - ple give thanks —— to the Lord. ——

Db/Ab   Ebm7   Absus   Ab

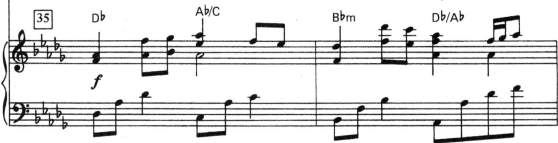

35

f

O give thanks un - to the Lord, —— sing His praise for - ev - er - more,

Al - le - lu - ia,

Db   Ab/C   Bbm   Db/Ab

—— praise the Lord —— for the things that He has done.

al - le - lu - ia,

Gb   Db/F   Ebm7   Ebm/Ab

AT THE CROSS

for S.A.(T.)B. voices, accompanied*

Words by
ISAAC WATTS (1674-1748) *and*
RALPH E. HUDSON

Tune: HUDSON *by*
RALPH E. HUDSON (1843-1901)
Arranged by
PATTI DRENNAN (ASCAP)

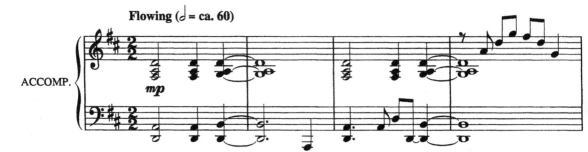

A - las, and did my Sav - ior

bleed, and __ did my __ Sov - 'reign __

die? _____ Would __ He de - vote that __

sa - cred __ head for sin - ners __ such as __

(end solo)

I? _____

At the __ cross, at the cross where I first __ saw the

BARITONE

light, and the bur-den of my heart rolled a-way.

It __ was there by __ faith I re-ceived my __

sight, and now I am hap-py all the

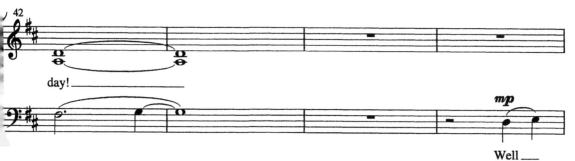

day! _____

Well __

might the _ sun in ___ dark - ness _ hide, and

But ___

drops   of ___ grief can ___ ne'er   re - pay   the

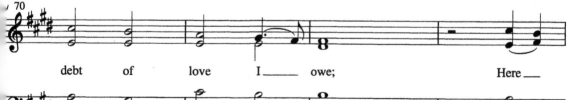

debt   of   love   I ___ owe;   Here ___

64

Lord, I give my-self a-way, 'tis

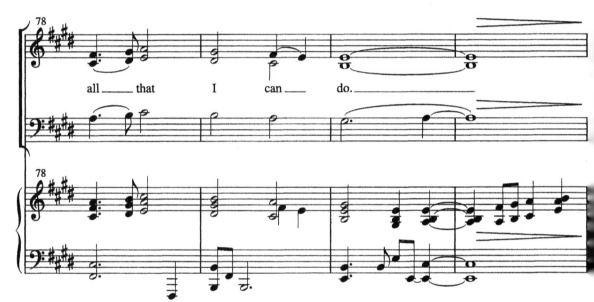

all that I can do.

At the cross, at the cross where I

first ___ saw the light, and the bur - den of my

heart rolled a - way. It ___ was

there by ___ faith I re - ceived my ___ sight and

now   I   am hap - py all   the

day,

at   the   cross.

GO IN LOVE

for S.A.B. voices, accompanied

Words by
DON BESIG *and* **NANCY PRICE** (ASCAP)

Music by
DON BESIG (ASCAP)

A5101

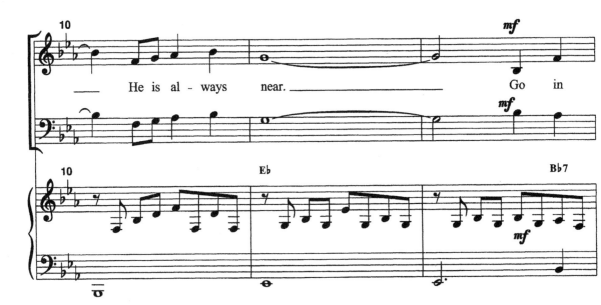

God will hear you, _____ He will un - der -

stand. _____ May His light for -

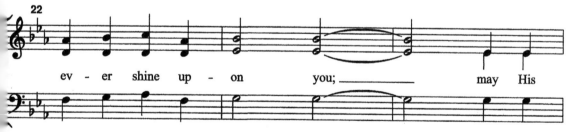

ev - er shine up - on you; _____ may His

peace be al-ways in your heart.

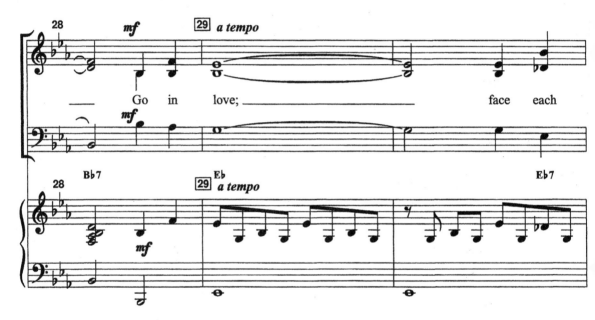

Go in love; face each

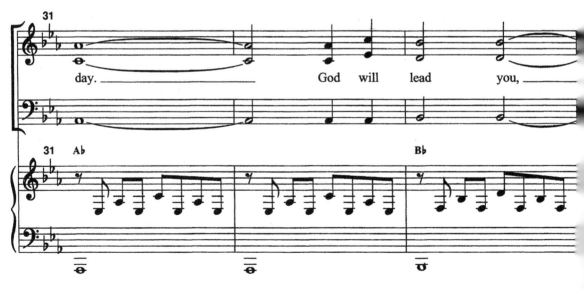

day. God will lead you,

He will show the way. Go in

love and live in faith. A -

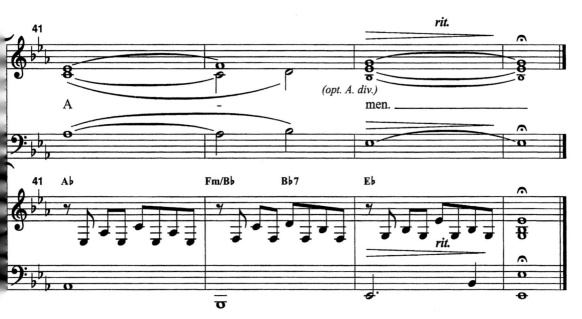

men.